EGGS OF WISDOM

A COLLECTION OF POEMS

RUSHI NIMMALA

Contents

Preface

Thanks to everyone who has helped me so far to complete this book. This book, 'Eggs of Wisdom' is a collection of poems which I have written between July and August of 2022. I was in a hurry for my studies, and I hardly got any time to write, but though, I wasn't able to abandon my habit of writing, I still try to write and complete a few things.

The title 'Eggs of Wisdom', is after the belief that, like an egg gives rise to life, I hope my poems shall be the eggs that sprout some wisdom, hence I named this collection thus.

1. Venom

I did close my eyes tight,
when my wandering mind fight
to seal and forget the sight
of that person with whom I might
or might not have a relation right
Like river flows the years,
Summer, winter and spring clears,
that person's voice still in my ears
shedding unnumbered tears,
until my memory bears.
After all that when shall I may,
return to those happy fields of hay,
a thunder shall fall on my way,
burning, consuming, taking me away,
from this world of ash and grey.
In the dark, I shall sit,
growing a treacherous, poisonous pit,
with fires of lies and betrayal lit,
with venom more dangerous than if a snake bit,
I gift it to the person for they deserve it
I shall fly like the butterfly free,
resting, staying and passing by the tree,

under the sun and cloud when flowers be
open and vast, colourful, and smooth as ghee
when rain flows, bathing and laughing I see

2. Unreal Garden

Little sparrows leap up high
And those thin twigs vibrate by
with chain of yellow flowers
the twine rising like tall towers,
chirping to wipe the tears and sorrow,
and this much beauty nothing can borrow
Red long millipede crawled,
with hundreds of thin red legs hauled,
on that wet floor as it rained,
and my heart forgot what it pained,
clouds fly by with cool air,
beauty filled my heart which was bare.
Squirrels ran over branch to branch,
squeaking and shaking the avalanche,
with butterflies flapping by,
among the pointy green grass and fly
over the high air with joy unreal,
Oh, it might be nice if such a garden is real!

3. The ocean is spread

(The ocean is spread)
With crinkly waves, spread up far,
Like a smooth road of tar,
Like a jam spread over bread,
Shiny as thin silky thread,
I must learn,
To keep on moving like the waves,
Whatever happens in life.
(The ocean is spread)
Under the sun like fresh cream,
Reflecting the warm sun's beam,
Cool and calm and froze like ice,
So much water than the knowledge of the wise,
I must learn,
To keep calm like the water,
Whatever happens in life.
(The ocean is spread)
Bearing the boats and ships very light,
At the glows of lighthouse bright,
Spread far like a vast liquid fire,
with winds faster than rolling tyre,
I must learn,

RUSHI NIMMALA

To bear the problems lightly,
Whatever happens in life.

• 5 •

4. When statues Speak

(When statues speak)
Poverty and suffering will vanish,
from this world of rape and ravish,
Robberies will cease with ease,
Making a society without evil and tease
No toxic human relations,
with no wishes and greetings of frustrations.
when statues speak,
No orphan will remain,
Love and Care will be the domain,
Beggars prosper and don't beg,
with foods like bread, milk and egg,
No cigar or alcohol is consumed,
with health and cleanliness bloomed.
when Statues Speak,
No guns at the terrorist's hands Battlegrounds turn into
grasslands,
No rape takes over women,
The world turns into a fresh linen
No knife bears blood,
Because love flows like a flood!
But only when Statues Speak!

5. Charlie wants a barley

It's raining, it's flooding,
The water drops are thudding
While the wheat is budding
Charlie wants the barley
And broke his head surely
By stepping into the puddle sorely
He lay on the bed all day,
seeing just rain but no sunray,
bored and annoyed all the may,
The raining stopped and sunlight came,
Spreading all the light soft and tame,
Charlie's heart grew high without blame.
With a deep feeling of joy,
Charlie dresses like a neat toy,
Remembering his days as a boy,
He grabbed his car keys
To buy barley and cheese,
By the dinner to make Harley please
It's hailing, it's raining
Icy stones from the sky refraining
Breaking the roof and windows disdaining,
An ice stone came and hit

Upon Charlie's head legit
And he fell therein with it
He lay on the bed all day,
seeing just rain but no sunray,
bored and annoyed all the may,
The raining stopped and sunlight came,
Spreading all the light soft and tame,
Charlie's heart grew high without blame.

6. O what can you?

O droplets of rain, can any of you bring me
A little bit of hope and sugar coated tea?
O fluffy white clouds, would you sing me a song
to wipe my tears which are flowing so long?
O endless sky, can you give me a little hope
From this despair and to quit this world a rope?
O formless air, can you blow away my sorrow
To have a glorious, delighted tomorrow,
O green leaves, will you bring me some bread
Of comfort from those unknown revenges red,
O brownish scarred woods, will you cast
A cover on me from those rains of memory vast,
O never turning back rivers, will you rinse my wound
Caused by those with whom I was falsely bound,
O tall, gallant mountain, will you shed a fountain
Of cool elixir in which I bath away all those stress I bounden

7. Hearts below trust

A rock of that mountain might melt,
But their heart was thin as a belt,
I fear I've overestimated them,
but their heart was a thorny stem,
What poison can compete it,
For their heart can make your throat slit,
Who knows what miseries hide
Inside in their heart's darkest side,
Their heart's filled with boiling
Acids and lustful liquids broiling,
Those are the hearts below trust...

8. Flower show

A shimmering lily, bloomed in the yard,
With little white cloak and a shiny green robe,
It turned up to the sky, and watched to infinity
Spreading pleasant smells all over the garden.
A grooming rose, blossomed in the yard,
With strawberry coloured jacket,
And waist full of thorn thicket,
And with green pajama pants fully fit for joy
A laughing Mary Gold, is born in the yard,
With a large turban made of gold,
Which would shine for the eternity,
And dancing through the winds all the town
An enraged Hibiscus, bloomed in the yard,
With face full red as if anger spread,
Wearing a mask of total red,
With green shawl sitting angrily at the corner
A silent sunflower, blossomed in the yard,
With face full of pimples of seeds,
Praying to the sun for removing those weeds,
With yellow scarf in the cold facing the sun

9. A road

A road that'll wind up to sky,
Away from the world and into clouds high,
A road that'll take me to magical cities,
Where hearts of men are full of graces and pities,
A road that'll lead to the cool moon's bosom,
I shall see first trees and flowers blossom,
A road that'll ride over Saturn's rings,
I will fly over there as bird with wings,
A road that'll cross the high realms,
I shall see god-messengers with great helms,
A road that'll fly away into the stars,
There could be various extra terrestrial wars,
A road, such a road, should be there,
And I should walk on it to somewhere...

10. What keeps me

My mind flays like a beast,
Hovering over the west and east,
To run and to come and stick with you,
I don't know what's pulling me,
Your thought fills me,
Your memory kills me,
Strangling my neck in the dark nights,
I want those days back,
Like a happiness filled sack,
Where have gone those days,
What took you from me?
Is it time, fate or our own treachery
Your eyes induce storms in me,
Your memories produce tears in my eyes,
I still feel a spark in us,
A hidden link of shock in us,
A strange force runs in our hearts,
What would keep us together?
After the manly things cut us and put us apart,
But I yet feel a spark in us,
One day it shall be lit!

11. Nothing

No, There's nothing,
Nothing here and with me,
I regret no one, and I owe no man,
I lay on those thin grass patches,
And breath free air,
I love no one hate no one,
All I know I must die my death alone,
And for that who can come with me,
I wish I had done this long time before,
Avoid loving someone and breath the winds,
Let my hair fly in the gentle breezes of the shore,
Truly, there's really nothing between you and me!

12. Smiles and Lies

Eyes are frozen like ice,
With unstoppable restless malice,
Under the curtains of dark thought,
More than what life taught,
My mind lay naked,
Hard like a brick baked,
The seed of blackness sprout,
Out came a sapling crooked and clout,
I am a man born and a man to die,
In the world where behind smile lies lie,
The saplings of wisdom wither,
Nothing can bring glow hither,
But Hope that we can get thither

13. Octopus

Wrinkly crinkly octopus,
Waits to get on the aqua-bus,
Off to school he will go,
With spongy shoes on his each toe,
Happy smiling he was,
And the exams he will pass,
Into the school he went,
Before the teacher he bent,
running shielding making fielding,
He played cricket,
Without a wicket,
Fatty hatty octopus,
Takes again the aqua-bus,
To home we went in fuss

14. Warm and Heat

The mighty sun blazed,
As to the east I gazed,
Gold and red rays spread,
A nice view to bite bread,
stars disappeared away,
by the yellow sun ray,
Clouds shined as snow,
With glittering lights in a row,
Birds hovering through fog,
Over the tall tree log,
Wind blew cold,
Hazy and bold,
Flowers opened wide,
Up came the bees for ride,
Sparrows came singing,
With bells ringing,
Ants creeped,
Squirrels leaped,
Vapour rose from my tea,
Forever this shall be...

15. The right moment

A day shall come when sun fades away,
When seas rise and leap above the bay,
When bird and beast cross the forest,
Run over the road and street without rest,
When the moon suddenly blasts
And it's large fragment on the earth casts,
When earth splits vomiting molten rock
The cities and towns burn without mock
When thunders kiss the barren lands
And fires hug the wooden tree bands,
When no one would live to see the sun rising tomorrow, for the
sun of humanity entirely sets into death,
Then will be the moment, when you and me, be without ego and
anger at the last breathe!

16. The sky summit

The dark cloud spread like jam
Upon a fresh baked bread with meat ham,
At the edge was a hole on the cloud group,
The mighty sun's face gleamed with a loop,
Orange and yellow rays scattered along the sky,
The nearby clouds glittered like fire high.
I looked at it in awe, it was the face of demigod
Looking from up above like a burning rod,
The delightful warm beam of the sun ran over the city,
Winds and clouds deviated without unity,
I pray to thee, O mighty sun, stay there ever,
Flourish the earth and life on it forever
I pray to thee to shed light with almost bright,
Until the tears of the innocent vanish from sight,
Shimmer your golden bright ray,
To grow on this barren land the yellow hay,
Let the trees prosper and grow,
People shall do the seeds of love sow!

Also By Rushi Nimmala

Fall of Godwin

Lost Visitors

Circular Squares (Anthology)

Tamil works:

Manathin Munaigal (Poetry)